ON THE BEAT

Jim Finn

First Published 2007 by Countyvise Limited,
14 Appin Road, Birkenhead, Wirral CH41 9HH.

Copyright © 2007 Jim Finn

The right of Jim Finn to be identified as the author of this work has been asserted by him in accordance with the Copyright, Design and Patents Act 1988.

British Library Cataloguing in Publication Data.
A catalogue record for this book is available from the British Library.

ISBN 978 1 901 231 83 0

All rights reserved. No part of this publication may be reproduced, stored in a retrieval system, or transmitted, in any other form, or by any other means, electronic, chemical, mechanic, photocopying, recording or otherwise, without the prior permission of the publisher.

FOREWORD

Jim Finn is still at it! Once a bobby always a bobby!

I was Jim's Section Sergeant when he first arrived at Lower Lane Police Station. Is it that long ago? It soon became obvious to his Sergeants and Inspectors that he had a lot to offer the service and he went on to prove them correct.

To my knowledge, this book only scratches the surface of the good work he put in to further his career as a serving police officer.

It is a good read and shows some of those lighter moments in a very serious occupation.

Bill Roberts
Retired Police Sergeant
Merseyside Police

Humour on the Beat

"What a great job this is!"

DEDICATION

This book is dedicated to all those police officers who, on a daily basis, steadfastly and diligently go about their duties in order to make our society a safer and better place in which to work and live.

Jim Finn

Humour on the Beat

"Laughter is the best medicine!"

JUST A COPPER

Often a hero sometimes a villain
Often condemned sometimes forgiven
A life that is held in lofty esteem
Liable to change on a whim of tomorrow
What of a role with intense dedication
That society feels a need to be changing
Perhaps one day the clouds will disperse
Recalling to mind the meaning of proper
Perhaps one day the sands will immerse
Enhancing in time the worth of a copper.

Jim Finn
2006

Humour on the Beat

"I think the licensee wants you off his premises!"

CONTENTS

1. FROM A PAIR OF BOOTS

2. TO A PANDA

3. PROMOTED SERGEANT

4. THEN OFF THE JOB

"Hey, Where are you going with my husband?"

Chapter One:
FROM A PAIR OF BOOTS

According to the words of "The Policeman's Song" from Gilbert and Sullivan's *"Pirates of Penzance,"* a policeman's lot is deemed to be not a happy one especially taking into consideration his relentless occupation with the likes of felons, burglars, drunks, juvenile delinquents and the rest of the unsavoury strata of society who make up the nether echelons of this world in which we live.

I served in the police from 1972 until 1986 and, in the pages that follow, I am going to debunk that notion by recounting just some of the more light hearted experiences I encountered during my constabulary duties.

Of course work is not all 'honey and roses' but being able to retain one's sense of humour when attending the more serious aspects of life on the beat, not only helps keep one's feet firmly on the ground and discharge one's duties in a more efficient manner but also gives the individual officer a more positive approach to the daily 'grind' of dealing with the public at large, with an additional bonus of cultivating a pleasanter personality in regard to other matters both on and off duty.

Hopefully, by the time you have finished reading the last page of this book, the very least I will have achieved is that you will agree that a policeman's lot is not altogether an unhappy one.

In actual fact my first connection with the police took place when I joined the Special Constabulary in December 1963. At the time I was working as a progress chaser (P.C?) in a large engineering factory on the outskirts of Liverpool. My working hours were 8am until 4.30pm Monday to Friday and so I had quite a bit of spare time on my hands.

One day, on the back of a bus, I saw a large notice with the words "Serve Your Community – Join the Special Constabulary" emblazoned upon it. After thinking about it for some time, I eventually went and I did and following a short course of tuition at Mather Avenue training centre, I was duly posted to the very busy Prescot Street, an old Victorian police station, complete with the traditional 'blue lamp' on the edge of Liverpool City Centre.

Specials are part time, unpaid auxiliary police officers, who wear almost the same uniform as regular police officers apart from the traditional helmet, a cap being worn instead. Each time we went on duty we were given the princely sum of six old pence (2½p) boot allowance and our travel expenses. Wow!

We patrolled on foot in pairs, no handcuffs, no radios, no pepper sprays, just a short baton and a whistle, on various beats throughout the Division, Wednesday and Friday evenings, and we also worked at the football matches, usually Liverpool F.C., on Saturday afternoons, the obvious advantage being able to enjoy the game free of charge despite dodging the half eaten meat pies and the toilet rolls that were thrown at us whilst walking round the pitch. We also performed duty at other major events that took place in and around the city, as and when required, for example the premier of the Beatles' film, "*A Hard Day's Night*".

I remember one time a colleague and I were standing in a shop doorway one evening on London Road, a main thoroughfare running into the city centre, when two youths came along and one of them hurled a brick through the window of a sweets and tobacconist's on the other side of the road. A smash and grab! We immediately took to our heels and after a short chase, caught one of them.

My colleague took the prisoner to the station whilst I stood by the shop window to await the keyholder. I had only been there a couple of minutes when a member of staff from the 'Prince of Wales' public house opposite came over and told me one of the customers was causing trouble in the pub. I abandoned my position and went over with him.

On entering the back room of the establishment I was confronted by a big Irishman shouting angrily, with a member of staff on each arm trying to drag him out of the pub and he was bouncing both of them up and down. I told them to leave go of him. He quietened down and I said.

"I'm afraid you'll have to leave. The licensee wants you off his premises."

He looked at me sheepishly. I placed my hand on his arm and began to walk him towards the door leading into the street. When we got outside I let go of his arm. He turned to me and said in his soft Irish brogue,

"Now you're not an ordinary policeman are you?" presumably because I was wearing a cap and not a helmet. I thought about it and replied, quite truthfully, "No," which was right because I was after all a 'Special' Constable.

He weighed me up and down for a moment or two and then said, "Well that's alright then, because if you were, you would never have got me out of that place as easy as you did." He then walked off, presumably to another pub. I was glad to see him go on his way and I resumed my position alongside the broken window.

Another occasion, I was on football duty at Liverpool's ground, Anfield, standing in one of the dug outs situated at various points around the pitch when one of the crowd ran onto the field heading towards the visitors' goalkeeper in a threatening manner, possibly because the goalkeeper had just pulled off a magnificent save preventing a certain Liverpool goal. I jumped from the dug out and ran towards him whereupon he turned tail and sped off whence he came. I was rapidly gaining ground and as I was just about to put my hand on the scruff of his neck, my legs buckled beneath me and, quite by accident, my hand caught the back of his heels and over he went, making it look like a perfect rugby tackle, much to the obvious delight of the roaring crowd as my cap went flying from the top of my head. By this time, two other police officers had got a hold on the culprit and he was escorted unceremoniously from the ground.

When I returned to my normal job the following Monday morning, one of my colleagues hastily approached.

"Hey," he said. "I saw you at the match on Saturday wearing a copper's uniform. What's all that about?"

I explained to him that I was a Special Constable and quite often did duty at the football matches.

"You kept that quiet," he said, "wait till I tell all the lads we've got a copper working with us" and off he went.

Within hours he'd spread all round the factory that I was a Special Constable and quite a few of them were not too happy about it. I became even more unpopular when one morning the local police set up a road block outside the factory and began to check everybody's vehicle excise licence as they were driving through the gates. The Production Manager was livid and lost no time in writing to the Chief Constable to complain about the cost of the hundreds of hours of lost production.

Anyway, I stuck it out for the time being until the spring of 1965 when I decided to call it a day and I enlisted in the Royal Air Force.

I served in the RAF Police in Aden in 1967 during the Emergency there and when Lieutenant Colonel Colin "Mad Mitch" Michell with the Argyle and Sutherland Highlanders restored law and order in the Crater district, after the killing of 22 British soldiers in one day.

I also served at RAF Ballykelly in Northern Ireland right up to the time of the first civil rights march which took place on 5 October 1968 after which the Province steadily descended into a state of civil chaos and murderous terrorist activity. I did stay in Northern Ireland for a while after my discharge from the RAF but when the Army moved in to take over responsibility for law and order in August 1969 I decided to return to Liverpool, my home town.

I suppose the idea of joining the Police was formed in my mind when I was about five or six years of age. At that particular time the fashion craze for young lads was to be the proud owner of a snake belt – a piece of elastic in two colours with the shape of a snake serving as the buckle, probably the equivalent in today's currency of a 'Nike' 'T' shirt.

After I'd saved up enough pennies and halfpennies to buy one, I went to the local park to show it off. Unfortunately, in the park were two no good louts who decided to relieve me of my much coveted accessory. One dropped down on his hands and knees behind me while the other pushed me violently in the chest. Over I went and within two seconds they had off my snake belt and ran away with it. I made my way to the park keeper's hut and in there was a parks policeman who, in those days, wore exactly the same uniform as regular police officers including the helmet, despite only being sworn in as Special Constables.

The Parks Policeman put down his mug of tea and led me by the hand around the park to see if we could spot the two offenders but to no avail. Disappointed, I thought maybe when I grow up I ought to become a Policeman. Maybe I'll catch the two robbers myself at a later date.

On Friday 1st December 1972 I was eventually sworn into Liverpool and Bootle Constabulary (which became Merseyside Police in 1974) by Alderman Sir Joseph Cleary. I felt as though my whole life had been but a preparation for that great moment and that great hour. In actual fact that was the third occasion I had pledged my loyalty to H. M. The Queen – the first time was when I joined the Special Constabulary and the second when I joined the RAF, all similar types of oaths of allegiance.

The following Sunday I travelled to the Police Training Centre, Bruche, near Warrington, to commence my 13 weeks training alongside 150/160 other recruits from all over the North West including North Wales and the Isle of Man. I was pleased to find that we were accommodated in single rooms and with the added benefit of a sink in each room things looked to be quite promising. But on the Monday morning, when I'd just finished shaving and I was getting ready to go over to the dining hall for breakfast, a knock came on the door and in walked a cleaning lady who began to dust round my room, I couldn't believe my eyes. I thought 'this is absolutely fabulous.' A huge step up from what I had been used to when I lived in RAF billets.

Probably because I was a mature entrant and having served in the Special Constabulary and the RAF Police and knowing a little bit about discipline, I was appointed not only Class Leader but also Drill Commander by our Instructor, Sergeant Joyce Mellor, much to the chagrin of a fellow classmate who was a former police cadet with Cheshire Constabulary. He believed for that reason, that he should have had at least one of the positions to which I had been appointed and he never stopped complaining about it on an almost daily basis.

However, one Friday, when we were many weeks into our training, he and I were paired off in a boxing match during one of our physical training sessions and we both laid into each other good style until both of us were in a state of collapse at the end of the bout. We shook hands and later went our separate ways on weekend leave.

On the Monday following, he didn't turn up to Bruche until lunchtime, it later transpired that he'd been to his dentist to have a couple of teeth pulled and also to his doctor to obtain a diet sheet which he had to present to the catering manager in order to go on a special diet. The upshot of all this was that he never opened his mouth again about my being Class Leader as well as the Drill Commander.

At the end of our 13 weeks of training I had the great privilege of leading the intake onto the parade ground for the passing out ceremony. We were lined up awaiting inspection by a very senior police officer and unfortunately he decided to make a bee line straight for me. I stood to attention. He looked me up and down.

"You're going to Manchester are you?" he asked.

"No Sir, Liverpool."

"Oh!" He then spotted the medal ribbon on my tunic which I'd got serving in Aden, "In the army were we?"

"No Sir, the RAF."

He looked straight at me.

"Where were you, Borneo?"

"No Sir, Aden," I replied.

He gave a low growl and walked off. Every question he asked me he got wrong. It was a good job I wasn't going to his force. There would have been nothing down for me.

My first 'nick' was the comparatively new Lower Lane Police Station in the Fazakerley area of Liverpool not very far from Aintree Racecourse, home of the famous Grand National. It was a very busy division with a wide range of police work and we covered both football grounds, Liverpool and Everton, two large hospitals, Walton and Fazakerley and also Walton Gaol.

In those days, as a probationer constable, you were posted to a beat and were expected to walk around it, with your Sergeant coming out from time to time to 'peg' you to make sure you were on it. We were equipped with radios which comprised two separate parts, a transmitter and a receiver, and so we were in constant contact with the Divisional Control Room. And of course, we also had the delightful job of school crossing patrols to do which were particularly rewarding in themselves usually in the form of a sticky sweet complete with the firmly attached pocket fluff.

I recall one morning I had just finished a school crossing patrol and was walking back to the station to get some breakfast. As I passed a particular bus stop, a local 'no mark' who was standing there, cupped his hand to his mouth and made a very loud, vulgar rasping sound. I wondered if that was meant for me so I turned on my heel and walked past the bus stop again. The same guy made exactly the same noise and so I went over to him. Words were exchanged and we ended up in a tussle. Both of us fell to the ground and I managed to pin him to the floor. Meanwhile, a woman pedestrian came over, started to slap me on the shoulders and tried to drag me off him. I called for a patrol car on my radio whereupon she rapidly disappeared.

Within minutes the police car arrived and we transported my prisoner to the station. It turned out that he was waiting for a bus to take him to the City Magistrates Court on another matter so, after verifying his details, he was discharged for Summons and off he went.

A few weeks later a Summons came through for 'my friend' charging him with disorderly behaviour which had to be served personally on him and so I got a lift to his home address from Swasie Turner, one of the more prolific Panda drivers.

I knocked at the door of the house whilst Swasie sat in the patrol car. As soon as the door was opened, the whole family came out, mother, father, brothers and sisters, as well as the defendant himself and I was surrounded by an angry mob demanding to know why 'chummie' was being taken to court yet again.

Within seconds, Swasie was by my side. He whispered something in the father's ears. Next minute the father punched his errant son in the face and ordered everybody back into the house. Swasie tapped me on the shoulder and jerked his head towards the car. We quickly got into the Panda and sped off down the road. I asked Swasie what had he said to the father. He replied,

"I told him that when his son was at the station he said 'this is all my father's fault, he is just one useless c___.'"
We both burst out laughing.

A few months later, whilst still a probationer and following a good number of arrests for crime, I was attached to the CID as an aide (assistant detective) for a period of four months.

One day I was in the office doing some paperwork when the phone rang. It was the Chief Security Officer from a local supermarket who informed me that a member of staff had been detained for theft as employee. I grabbed my coat and off I went.

On arriving at the scene I was shown to the manager's office. Sitting in a chair looking rather defiant though disconcerted, was the woman who tried to pull me off my prisoner at the bus stop all those many months ago. I thought 'this is my lucky day!'

When I joined the police we worked a cycle of three shifts – a week of nights, 11pm to 7am, a week of afternoon duty, 3pm to 11pm, followed by a week of mornings, 7am to 3pm, with two rotating rest days in each week, which meant that you were never on more than four shifts on the trot without a day off unless, of course, you were called upon to work your rest days at the enhanced rate of time and a half which seemed to come up with fairly regular frequency.

I used to break up my night duty by walking the beat for about half an hour and then stand on a junction for about

10 minutes surveying the scene around me. It was surprising how quickly the time went by working this modus operandi, especially during the first part of the watch.

One particular occasion, about one o'clock in the morning, I was standing on the junction of a main and side road alongside a piece of waste land when a finger of light darted across the side road which slowly widened into a shaft of light. I looked 50 yards down the road and saw the figure of a man emerge from the doorway of a house dragging a very heavy sack towards me. As he got closer I could see that the sack was full of bits of rubble, torn strips of wallpaper, lathe and plaster and so on. He was half crouched over the bag puffing and panting and gasping for breath. When he was just a few feet in front of me he stopped and stretched up to his full height in order to recover his composure before upturning the sack onto the piece of wasteland. He somehow sensed a presence behind him and turned sharply round. I was standing there in full uniform. In a flash, he grabbed the sack with both arms and fled back to the house in a record two seconds flat!

I witnessed a similar incident some years later when I was working at Copy Lane Police Station.

Copy Lane was situated on the edge of the sprawling Netherton housing estate. When Netherton was constructed, a new perimeter road was built around it which resulted in the adjacent country lane being blocked off to through traffic.

The downside of this was that a lot of household rubbish was dumped in the country lane, old mattresses, fridges, settees, etc., and I made it my business when returning to Copy Lane after a patrol to drive up and down on the off chance I might come across some of these nuisance fly tippers and one evening I did.

There it was. The proverbial white Ford Transit, rear doors wide open, full of bags of rubbish and nobody in sight. I got out of the police car and stood by the Transit. Minutes later, two men emerged from the bushes.

"OK," I said, "What are you doing?"

They both stared at me in disbelief. Quick as a flash the older one of the two replied,

"Oh, we had a couple of spare hours on our hands and we thought we'd do a bit of cleaning up around here."

I smiled and stood there while they did it.

Although, as I mentioned earlier, we were expected to stay on our beats, every now and again, one of the Panda drivers would come round and ask if you wanted to have a spin around the division, always a welcome break from pounding the beat as well as an opportunity to get some experience dealing with emergency and other types of calls requiring police attention.

One balmy summer's evening, whilst in the Fazakerley area, a Panda driven by Slim Watson pulled up alongside me. He asked me if I wanted to get on board and go for such a spin and I gladly accepted.

As we were quietly patrolling the Norris Green area, a vehicle came out of a pub car park right in front of us and the driver, upon seeing the police car, sped off. We caught up with the vehicle and pulled it to the side of the road. We checked both occupants and all seemed correct but it was customary at that particular time, whenever you stopped a vehicle, to always check the boot. It was packed tight with polythene bags containing umpteen cuts of chicken and steak.

Although both occupants worked for a wholesale butcher, they were unable to give a satisfactory account for their possession of these items so they were arrested and taken to Lower Lane Police Station.

Now, at that particular time, I lived with my wife in Skelmersdale New Town in the county of Lancashire some 15 miles outside of Liverpool. The reason I lived there was that when

I returned to Liverpool from Northern Ireland, being prepared to live in a New Town area was the quickest and easiest way of getting a house. Although it wasn't the most convenient place in which to live, we did have some very friendly neighbours.

Maggie who lived next door, every Friday evening, passed into us two steaks and two pieces of chicken for our weekend delectation. She said her husband was a chef in a pub in Kirkby and always brought home a large bag of such food items and we were thankful to her for her consideration.

Meanwhile, back at Lower Lane, we had got in touch with the owner of the wholesale butchers where our two likely lads were employed. On his arrival at the station, he took one look at the large consignment of meat and said that he did allow his staff to take home some of the produce but nothing like that amount. However, he did not wish to press any charges preferring to deal with the matter himself and so our two prisoners were released without charge.

When I finished work at 11pm I drove home and as soon as I got into the house the wife said that Maggie had called to say there was no meat this week as the two lads who usually came to the pub where her husband worked, had failed to turn up. I kept my counsel but needless to say, we never received any more chicken and steak from the well intentioned Maggie.

In due course I was posted to a beat on the tough Croxteth estate which, police wise, was a very demanding area. Apart from a few pubs and shops there was very little in the way of entertainment and amenities and the local teenagers were left very much to their own devices regarding how to spend their leisure time, which was not always of a law abiding nature.

One place of special interest to me was West Derby cemetery which was on the fringe of the Croxteth manor as this was where my best friend, Ron Brown, had been buried and his headstone on a number of occasions had been the target of mindless vandalism.

Ron had joined Liverpool City Police in 1960 and was probably instrumental in reinforcing my childhood ambition to become a police officer later on in life.

On Monday 19th February 1962, Ron was on night duty crewing a police land rover when at 6.40am, 20 minutes before they were due to go off duty, a 999 call was received to the effect that an intruder was on the roof of Endfield's garage in the Anfield area.

Ron and his colleagues raced to the scene and Ron being the keen and athletic person that he was, immediately climbed onto the roof of the garage to carry out a search. Unfortunately, the roof material was not of a very substantial standard and Ron crashed through it falling 30 feet to the ground below. He was dead on arrival at Broadgreen Hospital. The call turned out to be a hoax and the person who made it brought about the death of a young officer who had not only a promising police career in front of him but also the prospects of becoming a truly dedicated family man and a much valued member of society.

One day I was walking through the cemetery and I saw two 19 year old youths playing football using two of the headstones as goal posts. Taking umbrage at this, I went over to them, pointed out the errors of their ways and told them I would be summoning them for playing games in a public cemetery, although at the time I wasn't sure if there was such an offence on the statute.

When I got back to the station I pored over Moriarty's Police Law until I found the Cemeteries Clauses Act 1847 which fitted the criteria perfectly and summonses were duly sent out to the two culprits.

On the appointed day I was warned to attend the Magistrate's Court and both defendants were waiting outside No 1 Court. Unfortunately, there was quite a back log of cases for No 1 Court and one of the ushers came along and took a number of defendants from No 1 court along to No 3 court whose business for the morning had already been completed, one of whom was one of my defendants with the result that they ended up being split up and dealt with by two different sets of magistrates. It turned out that one was fined £1 in No 1 court and other £5 in No 3 court. So much for the equitableness of the English Legal System!

Many years later, after I had come out of the police. I was doing some work for a firm of Chartered Loss Adjusters, Colin Farley and Associates Ltd investigating claims for stolen motor vehicles and caravans throughout Liverpool and its surrounding areas, when I received a letter from the office asking me to contact another one of their agents in the Merseyside Area.

I met up with him at a café in Liverpool. It transpired that he was going on holiday and he wanted me to take over an urgent outstanding file for him, which I did, despite the enquiry being in a notorious block of flats in a less than savoury part of inner city Liverpool!

We got talking over our cup of coffee and this guy had served in Liverpool City Police the same time as Ron Brown. I asked him if he knew Ron. He looked at me with a deep anguish in his face.

"Do you know," he said, "that I was supposed to be on duty on the morning he got killed. We did a swop because I wanted the night off," he paused, shaking his head, "and I still feel bad about it even now."

That is a classic case of fate dealing a cruel and unexpected blow without the slightest ground for any justification whatsoever. But, unfortunately, the gift of being able to control our own destinies is something with which we have yet to be endowed.

Anyway, it was also whilst I was walking the beat in Croxteth that I got to know quite well the Chinese proprietor of a fish and chip shop. Originally from Hong Kong and having no known family, he had served continuously for many years in the British Merchant Navy as a cook acquiring for himself quite a sizeable amount of money. But, as time wore on, he found sailing the seven seas not as easy as it had been in the past and he decided to 'swallow the anchor' and bought this fish and chip shop in Croxteth.

However, after a few weeks, he totally regretted having done so. He ran the shop as a one man band and used to sleep on a bench in the back of the shop amongst all the sacks of potatoes, afraid to leave it unattended for any length of time for fear of break ins and vandalism.

I called into the shop one day and he had tears in his eyes. I asked him what was the matter.

"Bad boys throw stones," he said nervously, "make lots of trouble. No good." He looked very sad.

It appeared the local yobs were giving him a rough time, hurling abuse and throwing missiles into the shop on a regular daily basis.

From then on I made it my business to always call and see him when I was in the area and I would stand in the shop for a short while to give him some re-assurance. The situation did improve to some extent but eventually he felt as though he couldn't take it any more and he put the shop up for sale.

By this time I had well over 12 months on the job and I was sent on a driving course to the Force Training Centre where I earned 'my wings' by going on to qualify as a Panda driver.

"I'm not too heavy for you, am I Sarge?"

Chapter Two:
TO A PANDA

After completing my driver training I returned to Lower Lane and one of my first outings in charge of a Panda car was along the main road running alongside the Croxteth estate. But who did I see at a bus stop complete with his kit bag, none other than my Chinese friend from the fish and chip shop. I stopped the car.

"Where are you going?" I asked.

"I go to New York," he replied, a smile beaming right across his face.

I couldn't help but laugh. It sounded like he was getting a bus to take him all the way to the 'Big Apple' from that lowly, little bus stop, as if it was only a short hop away. He told me that he'd sold his shop to a Manchester based Chinese family and had decided to start a new way of life for himself in the United States. He'd booked a flight to New York and was actually on his way there and then to Liverpool Lime Street Station to catch a train to London. The worrying part was that he had all his money, probably thousands of pounds of it, stuffed in all different pockets about his body. If only the villains would have known that!

Anyway, rather than leave him alone in such a vulnerable position, I did what I could as a gesture of goodwill and I drove him a bit nearer to Lime Street in the police car. I just hoped he'd get to his destination without befalling any harm.

In Merseyside Police, in 1974, we had Minis for Pandas. Imagine that. Four big hairy bottomed coppers in a mini. The body of the car would be right down on its wheels. In actual fact I do remember one time when we were in the canteen enjoying our evening meal and a call for assistance from a colleague was received over the radio. Everyone piled out of the canteen, half eaten meals left on the tables, jumping into any available car. There were four burly coppers in my Panda, including myself, and I could only get about 10 miles per hour out of it despite my foot being hard down on the boards and all the exhortations of my very anxious passengers willing the car to go 'faster, faster, faster.'

Mind you there were many advantages as well as disadvantages in having Minis for pandas.

The obvious one of course was the ability to get down narrow back alleys to check the rears of business premises; off the beaten track to patrol 'out of the way' places and also to drive unobtrusively along the foot paths of large and open grassed areas.

I remember traversing a public park one hot summer's afternoon at about five miles per hour when I noticed some irregular shapes on the ground in the distance in front of me. As I got closer, there was an instantaneous frenzy of activity. I was able to discern several female forms, arms flying everywhere grabbing all manner of bra's and various colourful tops, sitting bolt upright and hastily dragging their clothes onto their upper bodies. By the time I reached them, they were all sitting quietly more than suitably attired. They smiled sweetly. I returned the smile. That was one of the more pleasant aspects of pro-active policing and I trust a good afternoon was had by all!

Another advantage was that if a Mini broke down, as they often did, due to their round the clock usage, you could put them under your arm and walk back to the station with them. Well, almost! Actually, one morning, I was transporting along with a colleague, two prisoners from Lower Lane Police Station to the City Magistrate's Court and on the way the Panda broke down at a set of traffic lights during the busy peak hour. I tried several times to re start the engine but without success. In the end my co-driver ordered the two prisoners out of the back and made them push the car. The engine burst into life. The two prisoners got back in and off we went to the hilarious laughing, clapping and cheering from all the people passing by.

We got to court without further mishap and after we handed over our prisoners to the custody staff, we thanked them for their help and co-operation and said that we hoped they would do alright in court.

One disadvantage was that a Mini was very easily turned over as I found to my cost one night during the wee small hours of a Sunday morning.

In the rural part of Fazakerley, tucked away behind the hospital, just off a country lane named Higher Lane, was situated a golf driving centre which belonged to the owner of a large sports shop in the city centre.

However, when he retired, a couple from Kirkby took over the golf driving centre, renamed it the Hickory Lodge and obtained, quite lawfully, a late night drinking licence. The result was that, after normal closing times in the pubs, a stream of cars and taxis would converge on the Hickory Lodge from all over the immediate and wider surrounding areas bringing scores of revellers to finish off their Saturday night jollification.

I was called to the Hickory Lodge at two o'clock one morning in answer to a report of theft and on my arrival many people were starting to leave and some of them were not too happy about the presence of a police uniform in the midst of their private little gathering.

I went inside and contacted the complainant who turned out to be Gerard Conteh, the brother of the former well known Liverpool boxer, John Conteh. Apparently he had left his newly acquired sheepskin coat in the club cloakroom and when he went to collect it before setting off for home, it had disappeared.

On hearing this, the two bouncers on the front door also disappeared and whilst I was halfway through completing the report, they came rushing, breathless, back into the club. One of them was holding aloft a smart very expensive looking sheepskin coat. It seemed that they had some idea as to who might have taken the coat and had gone after them in a car.

After stopping and telling the thieves who the coat belonged to, they immediately handed over the coat to the two bouncers and the thieves themselves then did a fast disappearing act.

Gerard Conteh immediately recognised it as his and after giving it the once over to make sure it was undamaged, he decided to withdraw his complaint and so I had to cancel the report.

However, when I left the premises, to my horror, I discovered my car was on its roof, my heart sank. I felt powerless to do anything about it.

Anyway, the two bouncers helped me put it back onto its four wheels but it was damaged down one side. I contacted the duty inspector who attended the scene and the vehicle was taken to the police garage for repair. I thought I'd have been grounded but no, I heard no more about it, that is until a few months later when the Hickory Lodge lost its late night drinking licence, after a stream of complaints from the local neighbourhood.

The beauty of being a Panda driver as opposed to a foot patrol officer was that it provided far greater opportunities to gain a much wider experience of dealing with emergency and non-urgent calls as well as the means for covering all four corners of the sub division and further beyond that.

Each type of shift was inherently different in its own right, even the first half of a shift, almost invariably, required a different policing approach to the second part.

For example, on morning duty, 7am to 3pm, the first part of the watch could be spent taking reports, one after another, of burglaries and stolen motor vehicles which had occurred overnight, whereas the second part could be spent checking abandoned motor vehicles, dealing with shop lifters, sudden deaths, dog bites and also serving summonses and that kind of thing.

On afternoon duty, 3pm to 11pm, the first part would be broadly similar to the latter part of the morning duty but after that the calls come in thick, fast and furious – youths causing annoyance, pub disturbances, reports of vandalism, assaults and robberies, stolen car chases, answering automatic alarms and of course, the inevitable domestic disputes, every copper's favourite.

The first part of night duty was generally an extension of the second part of afternoon duty but with more incidents of drunken behaviour to attend to. However, as night wore on, things usually began to get increasingly quiet and as dawn approached, there was relatively little else to do apart from wait patiently until 7am when we were able to get off home to a warm and welcoming bed.

It was during one of these quiet spells one night, about three o'clock in the morning, when Dave Jones and I were on patrol and we saw a rather posh looking Audi travelling a little over 40 miles per hour. Although the road was a dual carriageway the speed limit was actually only 30MPH but because of the lateness of the hour and the fact that we didn't have an awful lot on at the time, we decided to pull it over and check it out.

We pulled the vehicle to the side of the road and walked back to it. The window was wound down. There were two occupants sitting in the darkened shade.

"Good morning," I said to the driver, "do you know what the speed limit is on this road?"

"To be honest with you," came the reply, "I don't really know. It could be 30 or 40, I'm not really sure. I'm assuming it's 40 but I may be wrong."

The tone of the voice and its rapid delivery of words seemed somehow familiar and so I learned forward into the open window to get a better look. It was Ken Dodd with his lady friend. I said,

"Oh, good morning, Mr Dodd." I turned to Dave Jones. There was a long pause. We shrugged our shoulders. "Well, I suppose with it being a dual carriageway you could be forgiven for thinking it was a 40 mile limit."

"I'll remember that for next time," cut in Ken and he produced some publicity photographs of himself which he signed and handed over to us. We wished him and his lady friend a good night and off they went.

Now at that time Ken Dodd was doing a series during peak viewing time on Saturday nights on BBC television entitled "Ken Dodd's World of Laughter" which I always liked to watch and the following Saturday, being my weekend off, I switched on the TV to see it as was my usual custom.

Every week Ken Dodd would begin by walking out on stage equipped with his two tickling sticks and start talking for a few minutes about things which had happened to him during the week and on this particular Saturday he opened up by saying.

"I was driving through Liverpool the other night and I got pulled in by a Panda car and out got two Pandas."

I chuckled. I'm sure he was talking about Dave Jones and myself. And whilst we're on about celebrities, let me tell you about the time I met the legendary Liverpool Football Club Manager, Mr Bill Shankly.

There was a woman, her name escapes me, who ran a fruit and vegetable shop in Croxteth and she was a die hard, through and through, avid Liverpool supporter. Her effervescent nature, over the years, had made her a well known personality in football circles and she had become good friends with Bill Shankly. So much so, that whenever he was in the area, he would always make a point of calling into the shop to have a cup of tea with her and generally pass the time talking matters Liverpool.

One day I was in the near vicinity of the shop when I heard some kind of commotion and I went around the corner to investigate. Parked in a lay by alongside the row of shops was a very posh car. A man was standing by the driver's door with his back to me flailing his arms about. He was surrounded by a horde of young kids. Some were dragging at the sleeves of his coat whilst others were climbing onto the bonnet and the roof of the car so they could reach over the crowd to touch him.

As I got near, I could hear him shouting in his strong Scottish accent.

"Alright, lads, alright. Take it easy now. Take it easy, will you? Calm down. Calm down."

When he saw me behind him, he half turned towards me and cupped the back of his hand over his mouth, growling, gutturally.

"Get them off my f_____car will you? Get them off my f_____car!"

I ordered all the kids back off the car, those days the kids did what you told them, and whilst I was reproaching them for their excessive behaviour, Bill slipped into the fruit and veg shop and partook of a warm and welcoming cup of tea from Liverpool's number one fan.

Another incident which springs to mind also occurred during the quiet part of night duty, when I was riding 'shot gun' in the land rover, vernacularly known as the 'meat wagon', driven by a very experienced police officer, who had only recently come from the Traffic Division to Lower Lane. Not the usual way of doing things, it is normally the other way round, but, nevertheless, he seemed to be held in due high regard by the other Senior Constables on the watch.

Anyway, on this particularly cold and wintry night, the wind was howling and the rain was coming down in a steady downpour and as we were patrolling along the East Lancashire Road, the main arterial road running from Liverpool to Manchester, I noticed two individuals walking along, one behind the other, sticking their thumbs out hoping to hitch a lift in one of the slowly diminishing number of lorries and wagons going past.

They were not exactly dressed for the weather – short jackets, open necked shirts, loose fitting footwear, and so I asked my colleague to turn around the land rover while I checked them out.

One was from Liverpool and the other from Newcastle. They were both shivering and wringing wet. I asked them where they were going and they replied that they'd been to see relatives in Liverpool and were now trying to get back to Newcastle before the break of dawn.

The rain was still bucketing down and before I could ask any further questions, my mate elbowed me in the arm and said.

"Come on, let's get out of the rain," and proceeded to get back into the police vehicle.

As a parting shot, I blurted out to the smaller one of the two,

"Are you on the run?"
Through chattering teeth, he replied "Yeah."
I called back to my colleague and we put them in the back of the land rover. I think they were glad to get out of the rain and into the comparative warmth inside the vehicle.

Back at the station, after we gave them a hot drink, we found out from them which establishment they had absconded from. But when we contacted the prison to confirm their details, the staff there didn't even know they were missing. A quick head count at the prison proved otherwise and within minutes a message came tapping out on the telex machine reporting our two charges as being unlawfully at large. Now that is what you call quick work! Needless to say, my new found colleague never asked me to ride 'shotgun' with him again.

One of the most amusing encounters I experienced during my police career was when I was on afternoon duty in the Walton area of Liverpool.

Our Panda cars at that time, were not fitted with two tone horns or flashing lights. There were just two switches on the dashboard, one which illuminated the 'Police' sign on the roof of the car and the other, the 'Stop' sign.

It was about eight o'clock in the evening and I was stationary in a line of traffic on Walton Vale which is an integral part of the very busy A59. As its name suggests, it was, in the past, a narrow country lane and not designed to carry the volume of traffic that it now needed to do, hence the fact it was always severely congested with all manner of different vehicles including the occasional horse and cart.

As I was drumming my fingers on the steering wheel patiently waiting to move forward, my radio burst into life to the effect that the automatic alarm had activated at the nearby Hartley's jam works. I radioed back to say that I would attend.

I knocked down the switch on the dashboard to illuminate the 'Police' sign, pulled out of the line of traffic and sped off to Hartley's factory down the wrong side of the road.

I arrived there within minutes and as I jumped out of the Panda, a Morris Marina pulled in right behind me. Now at that time the CID did use Morris Marinas and when the lone occupant got out, assuming he was a detective, I shouted to him,

"You take the front and I'll take the rear!"

I checked out the rear of the premises and everything seemed to be OK, obviously a fault in the system which was most often the case with automatic alarms those days. The radio operator came back on the air and informed me that the key holder had been contacted and would be with me in five minutes, so I walked round to the front and spoke to my 'supporting officer'.

"Everything's all right at the back," I said, "you may as well resume."

"Resume?" he asked. "I thought you wanted me."

"Wanted you. What for?" I replied.

"I thought you wanted me for something."

"I'm not with you," I said, confused.

He then pointed to the sign on the roof of the Panda. It read 'Stop'. I had pushed down the wrong switch and believe it or not he had been behind me in the line of stationary traffic and had diligently followed me all the way from Walton Vale to Hartley's jam factory. Now that is what I call a very public spirited citizen!

I apologised to him profusely and he happily went on his way. After that I got some dynotape and placed the words 'STOP' and 'POLICE' under their respective switches on every Panda I subsequently drove to avoid any further embarrassment. But, to cap it all.

"Bravo Mike Two," went the radio. "Your key holder is en route."

"On the roof," I said. "What's he doing on the bloody roof?"

Another time on afternoon duty the Duty Inspector came on parade to address us before we went out on patrol.

"The Chief Superintendent is very concerned at the amount of graffiti that is starting to appear all over the place. He's had lots of letters from local people complaining about youths using these aerosols of paint plastering the area with names and cartoons on walls, fronts of shops and on the pavements

I've checked in the charge office over the last few months and there isn't any record of anybody ever having been arrested for this type of thing. It is criminal damage and as such there is a power of arrest. I cannot understand why nobody ever sees these offences being committed.

I want all patrols to keep their eyes peeled and pay particular attention to the likely areas where this kind of thing is more prevalent and if possible I would like something done about it today. Before the Chief Super goes off at five o'clock I'd like nothing better than to be able to go up and tell him that we've got somebody in for it. So, come on, let us be the first shift to get the ball rolling."

Twenty minutes later I was driving through the Norris Green area and I saw one such layabout doing exactly that – spraying a mural on the wall of the side of a shop. His back was towards me and he was totally engrossed in what he was doing.

I gently brought the Panda to a halt and walked quietly up behind him. He saw me when I was but a few yards from him. He hurled the aerosol down the road and began to break into a sprint. I shouted.

"No use running, I've got your fingerprints on the can."

He stopped and said he was sorry. I promptly arrested him and placed him in the back of the Panda. I then retrieved the aerosol and took him off to Lower Lane Police Station.

After relating the circumstances to the Station Sergeant, word got through to the Inspector's office that somebody had been brought in for the offence of graffiti and he came bounding down to the charge office with much enthusiasm.

Meanwhile, the Station Sergeant had asked the prisoner for his name and address and his surname turned out to be exactly the same as the Inspector's.

As soon as the Inspector walked into the charge office, he took one look at the prisoner, scowled and walked back out. Apparently the prisoner was a distant, though not distant enough for his liking, relative of the Duty Inspector!

I mentioned earlier the regular frequency with which we were called to settle domestic disputes and one such incident for some reason, always stands out in my mind.

Dave Mackenzie and I were alerted to an address in the Netherton area of Merseyside late one afternoon or early evening depending on one's own interpretation regarding the various times of the day.

On arriving at the scene we entered this neat terraced house with a nicely kept front garden. It was immediately obvious there had been a right old 'ding dong' of a row. Both man and woman were white faced and trembling with rage. We could see a soiled dinner plate on the floor and a sticky mess of gravy, meat and potato sticking unseemly to the wall.

Apparently the man of the house had been drinking all afternoon in a local hostelry, had got himself involved in some kind of argument and as a result, had come home in a foul mood.

Upon seeing this beautiful roast dinner on the table lovingly prepared by his dutiful wife, he had promptly picked it up in one hand and in a fit of pique, had slammed it up against the wall.

One word had led to another and because of his worsening behaviour his wife had decided to send for the police. We tried to calm the situation down but to no avail so we resorted to the 'Ways and Means Act' and enticed our quarry out of the house and into the street, where he continued to shout aggressively.

Without further ado, we placed him under arrest and into the back of the Panda. I got into the driver's seat and started the engine. As we moved slowly off, the wife came dashing out of the house and was running alongside the Panda banging her fist on the roof.

"Hey, where are you going," she wailed, "where are you going with my husband? Where are you taking him?"
We carried on and took him to the station, keeping him there until he sobered up and then we let him go.

Sometimes you just could not do right for doing wrong as far as domestic disputes were concerned and many police officers would dread going to them.

Being a Panda driver not only meant you were able to attend incidents very quickly, quite often offenders would be at or near the scene, but also, even after taking a report of crime, you had the means for carrying out any immediate follow up enquiries whilst the trail was comparatively warm and the perpetrators of the crime were still in a guilty frame of mind, which was always helpful in the obtaining of an early 'cough' statement.

As a result, following a long run of successful arrests and not yet out of my two year probation period and with most members of the CID dealing with one or more of my files, I was attached to the CID as an Aide (assistant detective).

Aides of course dealt with low end of the scale matters and I remember one occasion while in the CID office, my detective sergeant sent me downstairs to see the station sergeant.

After speaking with him for a moment or so, he introduced me to a man who was with his rather sheepish and very skinny 13 year old son. It transpired that the father, who was obviously a very honest and law abiding citizen, had gone into his son's bedroom and found all these budgies flying around. Further questioning revealed that his lad had stolen them from somebody's back garden shed and so his father had dragged him along to the police station. We did have a report for this crime and so were able to return the budgies to their rightful owner. The juvenile in due course, received a police caution and that, or so we thought, was the end of the matter.

Some time later, I attended the scene of a burglary where the lady of the house had been out shopping and on her return home, had discovered that an ornamental 'Flight of Birds' had disappeared from the wall of her hall way. There were no signs of any forced entry but she was adamant an intruder had been in even more so when she found some loose cash was missing from the top of her television set.

Because the 'budgie boy' lived in the next street I decided to make a visit. I told his father I was in the area and had called to see how they were. I also mentioned the burglary in the next road and left it at that.

The very next morning I reported for work and true to form, waiting for me in the station was the 'budgie boy' with his father who had a decorative 'Flight of Birds' ornament in a carrier bag. His lad was very co-operative and told us that he had entered the house by inserting his very skinny arm through the letter box and had turned the knob of the lock with his equally skinny fingers to open the front door. But, not only that, he also took us on a whistle stop tour of the Croxteth and Norris Green areas and pointed out a number of houses where he had done exactly the same thing, in the majority of cases, only taking any loose cash lying about the house. Eventually he was placed in the care of the Social Services and hopefully, his potential for a life of crime was nipped in the bud. I suppose if it wasn't for his fascination with birds, he might never have been caught and may have gone on to commit much worse offences for which he would no doubt, have been given a different sort of 'bird'.

Anyway, after four months in the CID, four commendations for good work in the detection of crime and a little over four years police experience, I was promoted to the rank of sergeant.

"That'll teach you to get locked up!"

Chapter 3:
PROMOTED SERGEANT

In February 1977 I was posted as a Patrol Sergeant to Tuebrook Police Station situated on the edge of Newsham Park, an area I was quite familiar with having been born and brought up in the near vicinity. The constables on my section couldn't understand how I knew so much about the lay of the land even though I'd only been there a few days. But I was keeping 'mum' about it. After all I needed some kind of an advantage over my troops. Knowledge is power and there was no harm in letting them play a guessing game for as long as it took me to earn their confidence.

It was a strange feeling taking my first parade as a Sergeant at a completely different police station reading out the beats, the refreshment times and any other items of interest to a group of officers I hadn't seen before, some of whom had far more years police service than I. I mean, only 24 hours earlier I had been a constable myself sitting in the parade room at Lower Lane with my Sergeant giving me the same sorts of instructions. I suppose that is what is known as becoming an 'overnight success'.

Tuebrook was in many ways, broadly similar in environment to Lower Lane, a densely populated area with plenty of pubs and social clubs with the exception of course, of the two football grounds and one of Her Majesty's prisons.

I recall one night reading out a communication to the parade to the effect that there had been a previous attempted burglary at Fairfield Conservative Club when several of the bricks in the rear wall had been forcibly removed. Possibly the offenders had been disturbed and had abandoned their project but the club officials, on discovering the problem the following morning, had at once engaged the services of a local bricklayer to re-set the bricks. Fearing the burglars would return whilst the mortar was still wet, the committee asked if we would give the premises special passing attention throughout the night. I assigned a recruit, 'Muff' Murphy, recently arrived from Bruche, to that particular beat and I arranged to meet him outside the front of the club at half past midnight.

We went round to the entry behind the club and counted the back entry doors as we went along until we thought we were in line with the yard of the premises in question. I tried the back entry door but it was bolted. Thinking that 'Muff' Murphy would be fit after just coming from the Police Training Centre, I told him to climb over the wall, unbolt the back entry door and let me in.

After several unsuccessful attempts to cock his leg over the wall, despite my propping him up and giving him a heave ho with my shoulders, he gave it up as a bad job and it ended up with me, the Sergeant almost twice his age, climbing over the wall and letting him, the recruit, in through the back entry door.

We checked the yard and everything appeared correct. I automatically tried the knob of the door leading into the building and it came open. In a bed was a couple copulating who, totally oblivious to my presence, just carried on with what they were doing. I quickly and quietly closed the door. We had the wrong place. It was the ground floor flat of the house next door to the Conservative Club. We beat a hasty retreat and when we eventually found the correct yard I instructed Murphy to check the premises every hour for the rest of the watch.

'Muff' Murphy didn't stay on the job very long after that and some time later, whilst off duty, I bumped into him in the City Centre, dressed in a smart grey suit. I asked him what

he was doing now and he said he was working as an electricity meter reader. I asked him what made him do a job like that and he replied,
"It's better than walking the streets!"
We both laughed.

Another time I was on nights in the wee small hours and a colleague and myself were on foot patrol on the streets in the Newsham Park area when we heard some kind of a disturbance taking place in the darkness of the shadows ahead. As we got closer to the source of the row, we saw a number of people outside a house and a male and female fighting and shouting in the road. We decided to investigate.

It transpired that a party was going on inside the house and a fight had broken out which had spilled out onto the street. The two people fighting in the road were the lady of the house, whose arm was actually encased in plaster of Paris, and her son who had apparently been the cause of the rumpus inside the house in the first place.

On our approach, most of the party goers went back inside the house but the mother, clearly the worse for drink and looking rather dishevelled, demanded that her son be arrested. As a result, because he continued shouting and swearing and attempting to push and shove his mother, I placed him under arrest for being drunk and disorderly and using threatening behaviour.

Normal practice on arresting an offender was to caution him/her by saying, as it was then, "You are not obliged to say anything unless you wish to do so but whatever you say may be taken down in writing and given in evidence." Whatever the offender said in reply to the caution could then be quoted in court. My charge replied,
"Are you stupid?"
In actual fact it was a lot stronger than that but that will do for the purpose of this text.

In due course the case went to trial in the Magistrates Court and when I gave my evidence I quoted the offender's reply in full. However, during my cross examination his advocate, a barrister no less, asked me for a second time what his client said in answer to my caution, after his arrest. Perhaps he didn't hear it the first time or he just wanted to hear it again so I replied in a fairly quiet voice.

"Are you stupid?"

The barrister looked at me impatiently and asked me to speak up. I said again in a much louder voice.

"Are you stupid?"

The elderly stipendiary nearly fell off his chair,

"What was that? Who said that? Who said that in my court room?" he barked.

"The defendant said that, your worship," I replied.

He looked at me with a penetrating stare, obviously annoyed, and said.

"I could have sworn it was your lips I saw move."

A muffled titter went round the court room.

As the Patrol Sergeant at Tuebrook I quite often had a police land rover at my disposal which I regularly used late evenings cruising around the streets keeping the street corner gangs constantly on the move. The mere sight of the land rover was enough to make them split up and go off in different directions and they would get tired of it long before we did. No need for any ASBO's then!

However, one summer evening I was out in the land rover driven by one of my constables when we were diverted to a domestic disturbance at a house in the predominantly flat land area of the sub division. On our arrival we were met by the female occupant of the flat and her occasional live in boyfriend. It was clear from their expressions and appearances that there had been a right 'humdinger' of a row.

As a rule, whenever I entered anybody's home I would remove my cap out of courtesy to the householder but on this occasion, when I saw the woman of the house close up, I kept it on. Her face looked familiar and she stared at me as if she was trying to place me from somewhere.

Anyway, we read the usual lesson and advised both parties as to their future behaviour and suggested that they try and resolve their differences in a more peaceful way. We further explained that if the trouble broke out again and we were called back, then we would have to arrest one or both of them and take them to the station to be kept in overnight, which usually was the man. Once we were satisfied that they had calmed down enough and had taken on board what we had to say, we bade them goodnight and took off in the land rover.

When we got to the bottom of the road it suddenly dawned on me who the lady of the house was. When I was four or five years old, she had been my baby sitter on a number of occasions when my parents had gone for an evening out. At the time she would have been a responsible 13 or 14 year old. I smiled. All those years ago she would probably have been slapping my legs and telling me to behave myself but now the shoe was on the other foot. I was pointing out to her the errors of her ways and advising her and her boyfriend as to their future conduct.

A similar sort of incident took place shortly after that but this time the person concerned was able to remember exactly who I was. Although I was a Patrol Sergeant at Tuebrook, when the Station Sergeant was on his day(s) off, I had to stand in for him as the officer in charge of the station which meant I was also responsible for the care and custody of any prisoners who may be brought in.

On this particular occasion I was on nights doing my station sergeant bit. It was just after two o'clock in the morning and the 'buzzer' sounded signalling that somebody had entered the station cell block area via the rear door. I immediately got to my feet, went through the connecting door and stood behind the tall counter on which rested the heavily bound charge register. All that was missing was the ink well and quill pen.

Along the corridor came one of the Panda drivers, minus his Panda of course, leading a male prisoner by the arm.

"Sergeant, I've arrested this man for providing me with a positive breath test," went on the officer.

"Name please," I asked the unfortunate one. He looked at me rather quizzically. There was a flicker of recognition in his face. He snapped his finger and thumb.

"Just a minute," he said, "don't I know you?" His face did look familiar. I had an idea who it was.

"Isn't your name Jim Finn?" he asked.
I nodded. It turned out that he was the guy who had 'shopped' me round the factory floor when I was a Special Constable all those years ago when I also worked as a progress chaser in the large engineering firm in north Liverpool before I joined the Royal Air Force. He asked in a soft, pleading voice,

"Can you do anything for me?"
I replied emphatically "No...o...o!"

On another occasion I was Station Sergeant at Tuebrook on nights when there was a vaguely similar sort of occurrence but this time I hadn't previously seen the person concerned but was to bump into her again at a later date.

This was also at approximately two o'clock in the morning but this time it was the bell on the front desk in the public part of the station that was pressed. A sweet young thing clad in her dressing gown and slippers, who lived nearby, was standing at the counter breathlessly asking in hushed tones if she could have a word with the Station Sergeant.

She told me that a cat was sitting at the top of a very tall tree outside her bedroom window meowing incessantly and she couldn't get to sleep. She thought it was crying because it couldn't get down from the tree and not only was she worried for the cat's welfare but also that she had to get up early in the morning to go to work.

I told her that I couldn't very well call out the fire brigade to attend a minor incident such as that. She appreciated that but wondered if I could go to the scene and try to coax the cat down from its lofty perch. I couldn't help but smile.

I told her I couldn't leave the station but the best thing she could do would be to put some smelly fish, like sardines or even salmon, onto a saucer at the bottom of the tree. I felt sure the cat would soon find its way down the tree and back onto the ground once the aroma wafted past its nostrils. She left the station as if a great burden had been lifted from her mind and feeling so much better for the advice given. I presume it must have worked because she didn't get back in touch.

However, a few years later, whilst working in Police Headquarters, I was standing in a queue in the canteen at lunchtime waiting to be served. Alongside me was a girl who I immediately recognised as the sweet young thing from Tuebrook. Apparently, she was a clerical assistant in Headquarters. I couldn't resist asking her if she was ordering fish and chips. I reminded her of the incident of some years before. She laughed and remembered that when she had got back home the cat had gone!

The advantages of being on night duty were that, in many respects, it was much quieter because senior management usually only worked days and there was less hassle from them, most shops and businesses and all schools were closed and traffic quite a bit lighter. But for one reason or another, the hours of darkness often seem to provide a catalyst to those people who are not at peace with themselves and choose to use this time to start acting out of character in all manner of different ways. The problem of course, is that when the police are confronted by a very tricky or delicate situation, the social and welfare agencies are only operating on a skeleton staff and those who have the responsibility for making executive decisions are nicely tucked up in bed. One such incident occurred one night in the period intervening Christmas and New Year.

It was five thirty in the morning and we had received a message from the Samaritans to the effect that they had been telephoned by a distressed female who was threatening to commit suicide. The call was traced to a house in Tuebrook and along I went with one of my Constables.

On arrival at the house we knocked loudly on the front door several times but were unable to get a reply. As a result, we knocked next door and a young Chinese man answered. He told us that the house next door was occupied by University students all of whom had gone home for the Christmas break with the exception of one girl whose parents lived all the way down in Cornwall. He said that he had spoken to the female occupant a couple of times during the week and she did seem quite depressed about being alone at Christmas. That was good enough for us.

We swiftly returned to the house next door and I gave it the benefit of my size 10 boot. The door crashed open and so did half of the wooden framework. As we entered the hallway we switched on our torches and saw the wall telephone dangling on the end of its lead. We checked the number on the telephone and found it matched the number given to us by the Samaritans. We gulped. We had a quick look downstairs and then started to cautiously climb the stairs to check the bedrooms, fully expecting to find a corpse in one of the beds. When we were halfway up the stairs, a sole figure wrapped in a white sheet, came gliding out of one of the bedrooms and sharply rapped.

"What are you doing in my house?"

We quickly recovered our composure and tried to ascertain if it was she who had phoned the Samaritans and despite the fact that her name was the same as that given to us by the Samaritans, she vehemently denied having done so.

In the end, she ordered us out of the house and showed us the front door. When she saw the damage she ranted that she was going to sue the Chief Constable for the cost of the repairs. I picked up part of the framework from the floor and said that the wood was rotten anyway and her landlord would have to fix it. I then proceeded to snap the piece of wood over my knee to prove the point but it didn't break. I tried a few more times but to no avail.

"There," she said, "I told you it wasn't rotten."

I consequently had to eat humble pie and I gave her the number of the police station for her to ring later that morning so that the police could call out a joiner to make good the damage. She was none too pleased.

At about 6.45am, 15 minutes before I was due to go off duty, I was walking back to the station when I was called up by the radio operator.

"The lady of the house you've just been to has asked me to thank you for your help and assistance and would like you to return to the house before you go off duty."

Needless to say, I carried on to Tuebrook, doffed my hat and coat and went straight home.

After two years at Tuebrook and passing the Inspectors Promotion exam, I was sent over to be the Sergeant in charge of a small brand new police station called Farnworth Street, some 20 minutes walk away but still an integral part of the Tuebrook sub division. In actual fact, Farnworth Street had replaced Prescot Street Police Station where I had served as a Special Constable in 1964/5 and was also a mere couple of hundred yards from the house in which I had been brought up. The immediate area around the station was now a completely open and flat wasteland of broken bricks and other builders' rubble awaiting housing redevelopment. It seemed like I had been half way round the world to end up back where I had originally started.

One of the last jobs I dealt with before I left Tuebrook was a series of complaints regarding criminal damage to a Morris Mini belonging to the occupant of a house on the perimeter of Newsham Park.

Several reports had passed across my desk over a short period of time, damage to the windscreen wipers one evening, a scratch down the side of the car another evening, meddling with wing mirrors another occasion and so on, with the result that I decided to pay the owner of the vehicle a visit.

She told me she was a barmaid at a local hostelry and worked most lunchtimes and evenings using the car to travel back and forth. She usually found the damage late the following morning when she went to get into the car to go to work. She refuted the possibility there was some kind of vendetta against her and couldn't for the life of her suggest any motive or who might be responsible for the attacks. I promised I would arrange some special attention to be given to the area during the times in question and I told her to contact the station if any further information came to light. The following week I moved to Farnworth Street.

Usually after the parade at Farnworth Street, I would wander through Newsham Park to Tuebrook to have a chat and a cuppa with the Duty Inspector and one particular night I was approaching the park perimeter when I was hailed by a gentleman walking his dog. He pointed out to me a vehicle on the edge of the park with the driver's door slightly open. He was of the opinion that the vehicle may have been abandoned and so I went over to investigate.

As I neared the vehicle I noticed a slight rocking motion and when I pulled open the door I encountered a male and female in a compromising position on the front passenger seat. The trouserless male immediately positioned himself into the drivers seat and I saw the female clad only in a waistcoat looking rather coy. It was the barmaid whose mini had suffered damage over the last couple of weeks. I advised them to park somewhere else a bit more private to which they readily agreed. As I walked away, it suddenly dawned on me what the possible motive may have been for the recent incidents of damage to her car.

The funny thing about Farnworth Street was that, although it wasn't all that far away from Tuebrook, it was fairly quiet during the day with most of it's 'moments' occurring on nights. I suppose, for the most part, that may have been due to the huge amount of demolition taking place in the area and the slow process of building the sprawl of new housing estates.

I remember one time on nights I gave the 'troops' on parade a 'penny lecture' about taking time to occasionally patrol the entries at the back of the rows of terraced houses still in existence, instead of sticking to the main roads all the time, maintaining that burglars and would be burglars didn't like to work out in the open where they could be seen, preferring to work under cover of darkness. One of my new recruits, Lou Beshoff, a rather tall, long legged young man, took me at my word.

It was about one thirty in the morning and I received a radio message to meet up with Lou at a particular junction, urgently. On arrival I was told by Beshoff that he had followed my advice and whilst walking past a half open rear door along one of the back entries he'd noticed a couple of brand new bicycles shining in the yard of the house.

On checking the bikes he seemed to think that they matched the descriptions of two cycles which had been stolen from a house in another part of the sub division a few days previously of which he had taken the report.

I requested another patrol to meet me at the rear of the premises and told Lou to 'hotfoot' it to the scene of the burglary and bring the man of the house back with him to identify the property.

Long legged individual that he was, Lou was back in no time accompanied by an excited and out of breath householder. He was delighted to confirm the bikes belonged to his two children. I immediately sent for another patrol to cover the front of the premises and asked for the night CID officer to attend.

On entering the house in question we were confronted by a veritable Aladdin's cave of all manner of stolen property although a thorough search of the house failed to turn up any of the occupants. In due course, all the property was removed by van to Farnworth Street Police Station and the team responsible for many of the burglaries in the Kensington and surrounding areas was arrested and put before the City Magistrates. A good evening's work and an example of what a recruit can achieve by listening carefully to what his or her Sergeant has to say!

Another occasion I was on duty in Farnworth Street and long after most ordinary people had retired to bed for the evening so they would be up and ready for work the following morning, the still of the night was disturbed by a gentle tapping noise on the front counter. I eased myself out of the Sergeant's chair, that was the one with the cushion on it, and asked the young man standing there if he needed any assistance.

With half a weak smile on his face, he told me he was a taxi driver and had just dropped off a young woman at one of the newly built houses opposite the station. Ostensibly, she had gone into the house to get some money for the fare but despite the taxi driver knocking several times for almost half an hour, she had failed to return to the front door. I donned my cap and went over.

I rapped on the door in a business like manner and shouted through the letter box in my most authoritative voice. "This is the police here. Can you open the door straight away?"

A few seconds later the young lady appeared at the door in her nightie and the taxi driver identified her as the miscreant bounder. I went into the house and explained to her that refusing to pay a taxi fare was an arrestable offence and unless she paid the required amount there and then, I would have no option but to take her into custody and put her before the magistrates later that morning.

She told me she had no money and looked rather forlorn. After giving the matter some careful thought for a few moments, she asked if she could have a private word with the taxi driver in the kitchen. Within the space of a minute, the taxi driver emerged from the kitchen with a bright gleam in his eye and a full smile on his face. He informed me that he had come to some arrangement with the woman and therefore did not wish to pursue the matter any further. He thanked me for my help and as I left the premises I heard the lock on the door click distinctively into place. I did notice that the taxi was parked outside the station for some time after that. Oh, well, all's well that ends well!

It was while I was at Farnworth Street that I heard the best excuse ever for somebody being late. Morning duty started at 7am and depending where you lived of course, some officers would have to get up at five in the morning whereas others who lived near the station would be able to lie in bed until the last minute.

On this particular occasion, one of the police women came in at twenty past seven and before I could say anything, she threw her arms in the air and said,

"I'm sorry I'm late but before you go on about it, you're not going to believe what happened to me."

"Try me," I said.

"Well," she said, "I got up at my usual time to get here for ten to seven but while I was in the bathroom cleaning my teeth a speck of toothpaste shot up from the toothbrush and hit me in the eye. My eye was all red and smarting and I couldn't see out of it for 20 minutes. I couldn't drive my car and that's why I'm 20 minutes late."

I couldn't help but smile. I looked at her not knowing whether to believe her or not.

"O.K," I said, "if you get your radio, I'll see you out on your beat a bit later," and off she went with an unsure look on her face.

However, about 10 years later, when I was off the job, I was cleaning my teeth one morning and the very same thing happened to me. A tiny speck of toothpaste shot up from the toothbrush and hit me in the eye and she was absolutely right. My eye smarted like hell and it was some 20 minutes before I was able to properly see out of it again.

The thing is I never saw the policewoman again to apologise for doubting her reason for being late all those years ago. It certainly was a case of her telling me the tooth, the whole tooth and nothing but the tooth.

It was also during my time at Farnworth Street that I was sent to Pannal Ash near Harrogate in North Yorkshire to train to become a qualified Police Instructor which is one of the best training courses I've ever been on both inside or outside the Police Service.

The course was very demanding and exacting and towards the end, it was usual to go to one of the Police Training Centres to do two weeks teaching practice and for an intermediate assessment as to your suitability to be a Police Instructor.

My teaching practice took place at Bruche, near Warrington, where I had trained as a recruit, and I remember quite well one day delivering a lesson on the Road Traffic Act (Construction and Use) Regulations. Everything was going without a hitch until I mentioned, with certain exceptions, that it was an offence to have a mascot on the front of a car. Almost immediately, one of the students shot up his hand and, peering over his spectacles, raised the question.

"Excuse me, Sergeant, what is a mascot?"

Rather surprised, I explained that it was a chrome metal object in the shape of a figure, often an animal or a bird, on the front of the bonnet of the car. I thought I had explained it reasonably OK but then the same student again put up his hand.

"Excuse me, Sergeant, where is the bonnet on a car?"

I looked at him with disbelief. I wasn't sure if he was winding me up or not. I told him as best I could and then asked him,

"Which force are you going to?"

"Merseyside," he replied.

I turned to one side and said to myself through gritted teeth, 'I hope you don't go to my section'.

Anyway, after my two weeks teaching practice I returned to Pannal Ash for my final assessment and at the end of the course I was very pleased to receive my certificate qualifying me as a Police Duty Instructor.

A few weeks later, following some weeks annual leave, I returned to Farnworth Street to commence morning duty. I strode into the parade room to give out the beats and other duties to the waiting personnel and, standing in line directly in front of me was 'my friend' from Bruche. He smiled. I groaned. He spoke.

"I'm glad I came on your section, sarge, it's nice to see you again."

I managed a smile.

After almost 18 months at Farnworth Street and sorting out all the old files and paperwork that had built up over a long period, it was decided to groom me for promotion to the rank of Inspector and in the Autumn of 1980, I was posted to the Organisation and Planning Department in Force Headquarters in order to get some experience of police administration.

Chapter 4:
THEN OFF THE JOB

When I joined the staff in late 1980, Merseyside Police Headquarters was housed in Hope Street in Liverpool City Centre just opposite the Philharmonic Hall, home of the Royal Liverpool Philharmonic Orchestra.

The building, previously a school for the blind, was a veritable warren of corridors, passageways, varying flights of steps and stairs, nooks and crannies and doors here, there and everywhere. How blind people found their way around I'll never know.

Following the formation of Merseyside Police in 1974, the increasing number of HQ personnel had eventually outgrown the available accommodation and working conditions became very cramped.

In actual fact, the room in which the Organisation and Planning Department was situated was a former corridor which had been converted into an office and was home to two inspectors, four sergeants and one constable and, with a door at each end of the office, there was a constant stream of people traffic going from one part of the building to the other.

Because of these severely cramped conditions, it was the dream of Ken Oxford, the then Chief Constable, to win funding from the Home Office for a brand new purpose built headquarters and in 1981 this dream became reality. Unfortunately, just as we were about to start moving into the new headquarters in Canning Place, just opposite where Albert Dock now is, the Toxteth riots broke out and everything was put on hold. Eventually, when we moved into the new building, there was a great air of excitement with the nicely laid out offices, brand new furniture, all the latest communications equipment and plenty of elbow room and wide windows which we could look out of, onto the world outside, most unlike Hope Street which was old, gloomy and almost devoid of natural light.

Because Canning Place was a modern purpose built Police headquarters, Senior Police Officers from other UK forces and overseas often came to view the building and its up to date amenities and facilities.

I remember being in the office one day when a member of the Chief Constable's staff came in with three foreign police dignitaries one of whom was from the Yemen, which is where Aden is situated, in the Middle East. I couldn't resist telling him that I had served in the RAF Police in Aden in 1967 and I asked him what happened to all the pro British Sheikhs and Sultans after we pulled out, handing over administration of the colony to the National Liberation Front. He smiled glistening white teeth and gently drew his right forefinger sharply across his throat. I winced. A vivid flashback immediately passed across my mind.

When I was in Aden all those years ago, the billet I slept in was on high ground and it was quite a long walk to the guardroom where we would parade for duty each day and pick up a Smith and Wesson revolver and 12 rounds of ammunition.

On this particular day, I was feeling rather tired and, dressed in full uniform with my belt, cross strap and empty holster over my shoulder, I decided to hitch a lift, so I stopped a high sided truck which was going my way.

Because there were three local nationals already in the cab, I swung myself over the side boards into the back of the truck where I was confronted by about 15 Arabs all in various sleeping positions, obviously some kind of work party. I panicked. I suddenly felt very unsafe, particularly when some of them began to wake up and fix their eyes upon me. Before

I could jump out of the truck, the driver sped off. I remained standing with my head and shoulders above the side boards and as soon as the guardroom came in sight I banged on the roof of the cab shouting,

"This'll do fine. This'll do fine."

Fortunately the vehicle pulled to a halt and I jumped off with a huge sigh of relief. I had visions of being taken up country and never being seen again. Phew!

Once all HQ departments had finally moved out of Hope Street and got settled into Canning Place, an executive decision was made to change the format of the police promotion boards. Whereas, prior to joining the Organisation and Planning Department, I had already passed the Inspectors Promotion Board, it now became necessary for me to go before another Board under the new system and disaster struck.

The findings of the Board were 'that an officer of his experience should have answered the questions better and that he should return to a division for further street experience.' It didn't make sense really because the first part of the statement acknowledged I had the experience but then the latter part indicated I needed some more?

However, in due course, November 1982 to be precise, I was posted back in uniform to Copy Lane Police Station which covered quite a wide area including Aintree Race Course, home of the Grand National, and Ashworth top security hospital, working the streets on three shifts.

My first duty on arriving at Copy Lane was on nights and at 11pm when I entered the parade room to address my new section, I spotted amongst the sea of unfamiliar faces the unmistakable countenance of my very good friend and protégé from Bruche and Farnworth Street, the guy who didn't know the difference between a bonnet and a boot lid on a car and a mascot from a gasket. I was speechless.

"Hi, Sarge," said he.

I didn't know whether to laugh or cry. The words 'bad penny' quickly came to mind.

Copy Lane was an irregular station in so far as there was no common denominator to the place. Personnel there were from all over Liverpool, Bootle, Southport, St. Helens, Lancashire, Wirral and Cheshire, with the result there appeared to be a marked lack of cohesion in working relationships right across the board and morale was not very high.

Still, police work is police work and that's what the job is supposed to be all about. Word soon spread round certain quarters, not all, that I had been sent from Headquarters to sort the place out.

I must admit I did find that the attitudes of new recruits coming into the job seemed to have considerably changed during the two years I had been ensconced in Force Headquarters.

One occasion which sticks in my mind was when one of the probationers who had only been with me a few weeks asked me if he could borrow my uniform for the weekend because his father was going to a fancy dress party on the Saturday night and he wanted to go dressed as a Police Sergeant rather than a 'lowly' Police Constable. Was I hearing things?

Needless to say, I made my feelings known to him and pointed out the reverence he should have for the cloth to which I hoped he would henceforth subscribe but I'm not sure if he thought I was pulling his leg, just as I thought he was pulling mine when he made his request in the first place.

However, after three years of regularly and diligently carrying out acting Inspector duties and sailing through my eventual follow up promotion board with flying colours, my police career, unfortunately, came to an untimely end.

Following physiotherapy at the police convalescent home in Harrogate for a back injury sustained whilst trying to kick in a door to a block of flats where a distraught female was threatening to throw herself out of a first floor window, I was summoned to appear before Professor Semple, the Medical Officer of Health. He recommended I go off the job on medical grounds and on 7 July 1986, after being interviewed by Alison Halford, the Assistant Chief Constable for Personnel, I eventually received my discharge certificate and I had to hand in my police warrant card.

I remember returning to the station for the last time in order to clean out my locker and in so doing I noticed a white envelope on the top shelf which I put into my pocket for when I got home. From memory, the contents read,

"It is not the critic who counts
nor the lesser mortal who points
to the doer of good deeds
who may occasionally stumble.
The credit belongs to the one
Who is out there in the arena
getting the blood, the sweat, the tears
and the dirt on his face.
His place is not with those
who have never known victory or defeat
but with those who have tried
and if they failed
at least failed whilst daring greatly."

However, that was not the end of policing as far as I was concerned because in no time at all I secured for myself a position with Foster Bros (Central Services) Ltd as an Audit/ Security Investigator which was one of the best jobs I've ever had. I was allocated a company car and an expense account, something I'd always dreamed about, and worked from home looking after over 100 retail outlets – Foster Menswear, Your

Price, Adam's Children's wear etc. covering every major city and town throughout the North West and North Wales, including Anglesey.

I remember one afternoon attending one of our shops in Birkenhead where a small amount of money had gone missing from the till. After closely examining the transactions on the till roll, all the evidence pointed to one particular individual who, after questioning, admitted responsibility for the theft.

The police were informed and in due course the local beat constable attended the shop. He put his helmet on the table in the staff room and after listening to the circumstances he said, unabashed,

"Look, it's my birthday today and I'm due off at three o'clock. I've arranged with all the lads from the section to go for a pint after work. Do you mind if I just give him a Police Caution?"

My mouth dropped. I was lost for words for a few moments and then said,

"Well, actually, I've been on to Head Office and they want the matter to go to court."

With great reluctance, he led the culprit by the arm out of the shop towards the police car waiting outside. I politely wished him 'happy birthday' and off they went. I couldn't help but smile. I'd only been off the job a couple of years and the face of traditional policing, for better or for worse, seemed to be changing already, forever.

Mind you, not every investigation ended up with somebody appearing before the courts and possibly losing their job, sometimes the reverse was equally the case.

It was a Tuesday and I had been routinely visiting some outlets in the North Wales area but because I'd got round them pretty quickly, I decided to stop off at Chester on my way home and finish the day at a couple of shops there.

As soon as I entered the first shop in Chester, I immediately detected an urgent sense of alarm and despondency. Apparently, a few days previously, a routine stock audit had been carried out and it was found that there was a stock shortage to the tune of £4000.

The shop manager was overwrought with anxiety, the Regional Manager was coming to see him the following day and he was fully expected to get the sack. But, not only that, all the staff had been told they were being paid no bonus despite all the efforts they had put in to boost the sales over the past few months and their mood was not exactly friendly.

I knew the manager from another shop he'd previously run, and I thought he was a decent type, so I took off my coat, rolled up my sleeves and instructed him to do the same. I told him we were going to scrutinise with a fine tooth comb, every single piece of paperwork in the shop relating to the period in question.

At first, feeling demotivated and rather dejected, he was reluctant to do so but following some gentle persuasion, I eventually, talked him round.

After about an hour of checking every word on every line of every single document, 'Eureka!' we found a delivery note in that sum of money which referred to a consignment of goods that had arrived at Chester some weeks ago but, in fact, had never been unloaded, instead, diverted to another branch in Oldham.

The manager nearly jumped the size of himself. He flew out of the office onto the shop floor, holding aloft the piece of paper in his hand, clicking his heels in great excitement. The infectious joy quickly spread to all members of staff and broad, beaming smiles returned to their faces once again. There were celebrations all round and I left the shop to many 'thank you's' and feeling quite pleased with myself.

I found out some days later that after the Regional Manager's visit the following day, not only was the staff bonus re-instated but also my friend, the manager, received a steep increase in his salary.

I never did get round to calling back to the shop to pick up my promised bottle of whisky because it was shortly after that, that I decided to resign my position with Foster Bros and go on to pastures new.

Although I came out of Merseyside Police in 1986 I still kept some links with the job by remaining a key member of the Police Concert Party right up to 2001.

The Police Concert Party was run and compered by Alan Roberts ably assisted by the hilarious Brian "I've found me bike" McDonald, a very funny man indeed. It consisted of serving and retired police officers, talented in one way or another, who freely gave of their spare time to entertain all kinds of different audiences at residential homes, community centres, church halls, hospitals and the like, all over Merseyside, Wirral, West Lancashire and parts of Cheshire. There was guitar vocalist Dave Dundas who I suppose could be described as a scouse Jasper Carrott and of course, our very own nightingale of song, Miss Sandra Dean, who gave a great account of herself singing popular evergreens and songs from shows. I did a bit with my guitar covering Lonnie Donegan songs mainly "Putting on the style," and "My old man's a dustman" but the number I most often requested to do was for the old time favourite, "My brother, Sylveste."

When I was doing my basic training at Bruche in 1972/3, it was customary for the outgoing intake during their last week of training to put on a concert referred to as a 'Ram Sami' for the senior officers and the rest of the staff and students.

However, when it became our turn to put on a show, I just didn't know what I was going to do. Then one day as I was walking through the accommodation block, I saw a member of our class sitting on his bed playing a guitar. I asked him for a go of his guitar and after doing a couple of numbers, it was there and then decided what I was going to do for the 'Ram Sami'.

When the evening finally arrived, everything went off very well. I came on stage towards the end and did a Johnny Cash number, "Austin Prison" followed by Lonnie Donegan's "Battle of New Orleans." The 'tumultuous' applause was so enthusiastic that within weeks of leaving Bruche, I made a point of buying myself a 'Ranger 6' acoustic/electric guitar and set about teaching myself a much wider repertoire.

Even so, it was not until 1978, the year after I was promoted Sergeant, that I spotted a small piece in Force Orders asking for anybody who could entertain and fancied joining the Police Concert Party to ring a particular phone extension number.

After much thought and deliberation, I eventually decided to give it a shot and the voice at the other end of the telephone line was the unmistakably resonant voice of Alan Roberts who actually persuaded me to go along to a show that very evening and see for myself what it was all about. I did and I was very impressed.

I first met Alan Roberts in 1973. I hadn't been out of Bruche very long and one particular night at about two thirty in the morning I was standing in a shop doorway on Walton Vale. The rain was absolutely bucketing down and I was wondering how I was going to get back to Lower Lane for refreshments without getting soaking wet. Just then, out of the blue, a mini van came from the other side of the road and pulled alongside the kerb in front of me. I thought 'Hello, this looks like trouble' and walked over to the driver. He wound down the window and I could see his blue police shirt and black tie. He was on his way home after finishing a tour of duty on the other side of the city.

He said,

"I only live down the road, do you want to jump in and go for a cuppa?"

"I have to be back in the station for three o'clock for my refreshments," I said.

"That's OK," replied Alan, "I'll take you back there for three."

I went home with him where his wife, Kay, supplied us with copious amounts of steaming hot cocoa and soup. I soon filled my boots and Alan ran me back to Lower Lane. After he dropped me off at the station, I thought to myself 'What a great guy he is' with the result that when he answered the phone regarding my enquiry about joining the Police Concert Party, I needed very little persuasion to do so.

Part of my routine whilst doing my act with the Police Concert Party was to sing a couple of numbers and then pull out a piece of paper from my pocket, from which I would read, "I have a request here for Elsie who's 111. Is she in?" I'd look around the audience and repeat, "Elsie who's 111. Is she in?" Everybody would look around at each other trying to spot who was 111 years of age but after half a minute or so I would stop and say,

"Oh, hang on. I'm awfully sorry, it's not Elsie who's 111, it's Elsie who's ill. Sorry about that. That's obviously why she's not here. Anyway, this one is for Elsie and let's hope she gets better soon." I would then carry on with the next song.

However, on one particular occasion, after going through the Elsie routine, I noticed an elderly lady at the back of the hall coming slowly down the room towards me on her zimmer. I thought she was probably making her way to the toilet but by the time I had finished my rendition, she was standing alongside and looking up at me. I asked her if she was alright and she replied in a very quiet voice,

"Did you want me?" I looked at her askance.

"I thought you wanted me," she said.

"Want you, love?" I asked rather bewildered, "What would that be for?"

"My name's Elsie," she replied," you asked for me. I thought you wanted me."

"Oh, yes," I said, completely bowled over. I thanked her for coming down to the front to see me and after getting the audience to give her a good round of applause I, of course, dedicated the next song to her.

One venue with the Police Concert Party that sticks out in my mind is the Caribbean Community Centre in the Toxteth area of Liverpool.

Toxteth comprised many diverse ethnic minorities and there had always been a long tradition of intermittent uneasiness between some of the residents and the police which at times led to feelings of distrust and extreme resentment running rather high.

In the summer of 1981, a flashpoint took place which developed into large scale street disorder and fierce fighting between various factions and Merseyside Police. The situation became almost impossible to contain and a number of 'no go' areas were quickly established by riotous gangs.

As a result, contingents from police forces all over the country descended upon Liverpool saturating the Toxteth area in order to maintain some resemblance of law and order.

Once a comparative peace and calm had been restored, all the assisting forces returned to their own areas whilst Merseyside Police swiftly set up a variety of bridge building initiatives to try and repair the damage that had caused the serious breakdown in community relations.

One such initiative involved sending members of the Police Band and the Concert Party into Caribbean Club in order to entertain the local populace. It wasn't easy. Tensions were still running very high and it was considered a good idea, an idea to which we all fully subscribed, to have two vans of suitably equipped police personnel located in the near vicinity of the club.

Quite a few of the local people, although a bit suspicious of any ulterior motives, turned up to see us but you could have cut the atmosphere with the proverbial knife. We didn't seem to make much of an impact on the audience, perhaps they were reluctant to show it, and after I did my spot, I think it was the only time I ever walked off a stage to the sound of my own footsteps.

However, we persevered with our endeavours and the general consensus was that we had assisted in some small way, to lay the foundations on which it became possible to build a new and better understanding of each other's cultures.

In due course, normal policing was resumed as soon as it was safe to do so and I like to think that the Police Concert Party may have had some hand in helping to bring this about.

At the start of this book, I began by summarising the contents of "The Policeman's Song" from Gilbert and Sullivan's the Pirates of Penzance. The nature of the duties as a Constable is accordingly made out to be one of constantly dealing with thieves, cut throats, drunks, juvenile delinquents and so on, emphasising all the way through the song that 'a Policeman's lot is not a happy one'.

I also made the statement that by the end of the book I hoped I would be able to dispel this misrepresentation of a policeman's lot and instead paint a truer picture that life on the beat is never dull and, in fact, can be richly rewarding, indeed enjoyable, it depends entirely on the calibre of each individual officer's character, personality, attitude and zest for the job.

I must admit my reading over the pages of the book has not only brought back many a happy and pleasant memory but also, several times, raised more than just a tiny titter or cheery chuckle.

I would therefore like to end by quoting from a popular music hall song also from yesteryear entitled "The Laughing Policeman" in which the world and his wife are of the considered opinion that a Policeman (or woman) for that matter is, in fact, the happiest man (woman) in town!

<u>ET PRO QUO EST</u>

"The boss said we could take some meat home for our Sunday dinner!"

INDEX

	Page
Aden	14, 60
Aintree Race Course	17
Alan Roberts	66, 67
Albert Dock, Liverpool	59
Alderman Sir Joseph Cleary	15
Assistant Chief Constable Alison Halford	63
A Policeman's Lot is Not a Happy One	11
Argyle and Sutherland Highlanders	14
Ashworth Hospital Merseyside	61
Bill Shankly	32, 33
Birkenhead	64
Brian McDonald	66
Broad Green Hospital Liverpool	23
Bruche, Warrington	16, 17, 44, 56, 66
Canning Place, Liverpool	59, 60, 61
Caribbean Community Centre, Liverpool	69
Cemeteries Clauses Act 1847	23
Cheshire Constabulary	16
Chester	64, 65
CID Aide	19, 39
Colin Farley and Associates Ltd	24
Copy Lane Police Station Netherton	20, 61, 62
Croxteth, Liverpool	22, 24, 25, 27, 40
Dave Dundas	66
Dave Jones	31, 32
Dave Mackenzie	38
Endfields of Anfield	23
Everton F.C.	17

Fairfield Conservative Club	43, 44
Fazakerley Hospital, Liverpool	17
Farnworth Street Police Station	51, 52, 53, 54, 55, 57
Foster Bros (Central Services) Ltd	63, 66
Gerard Conteh	29, 30
Hartley's Jam Works	35, 36
Hickory Lodge, Fazakerley	29, 30
Hope Street, Liverpool	59, 60
Inspector's Promotion Board	61
Johnny Cash	67
Kay Roberts	68
Ken Dodd	32
Ken Oxford, Chief Constable	59
Kensington, Liverpool	54
Lieutenant Colonel Colin Mitchell	14
Liverpool and Bootle Constabulary	15
Liverpool F.C	12, 32
Liverpool Lime Street Railway Station	27
Liverpool Magistrates Court	18, 23, 28, 46
Lonnie Donegan	66
Lou Beshoff	53, 54
Lower Lane Police Station, Fazakerley	17, 21, 22, 27, 28, 33, 37, 43, 67
Maggie	22
Mather Avenue Training Centre	12
Merchant Navy	25
Merseyside Police	15, 27, 59, 66, 69
'Muff' Murphy	44
National Liberation Front	60
Netherton	38
Norris Green	21, 37, 40

Northern Ireland	15, 22
Oath of allegiance	16
Organisation and Planning Department	58, 59
Parks Policeman	15
Police Concert Party	66, 67, 68, 69, 70
Police Convalescent Home, Harrogate	62
Police Headquarters	49, 59
Police Station, Prescot Street	12, 51
Prince of Wales Public House	13
Professor Semple	63
RAF Ballykelly	15
Ram Sami	66, 67
Ron Brown	22, 23, 24
Royal Air Force Police	14, 16, 60
Royal Liverpool Philharmonic Orchestra	59
Samaritans	50
Sandra Dean	66
Sergeant Joyce Mellor	16
Skelmersdale New Town, Lancashire	21
Slim Watson	21
Snake Belt	15
Special Constabulary	11, 12
Swasie Turner	18, 19
The Laughing Policeman	71
The Pirates of Penzance	11
Toxteth, Liverpool	59, 69
Tuebrook Police Station	43, 46, 47, 48, 51, 52
Walton Gaol	17
Walton Hospital	17
Walton Vale, Walton	35, 36, 67
West Derby Cemetery, Liverpool	22

ABOUT THE AUTHOR

Jim Finn began his law enforcement career at the age of eleven when he was appointed a prefect at Newsham County Primary School, Liverpool, in 1954. Nine years later he joined Liverpool City Police Special Constabulary and was posted to Prescot Street Police Station on the edge of Liverpool City Centre.

In 1965 he signed on the dotted line and joined the Armed Forces serving as an RAF Policeman at Ballykelly in Northern Ireland and at Steamer Point during the latter days of the Aden Emergency in 1967.

In 1972 Jim achieved his childhood ambition when he was sworn into Liverpool and Bootle Constabulary, as a regular police officer, which later became Merseyside Police.

Following early retirement in 1986 in the rank of acting Inspector, he went on to work as an Audit/Security Investigator with Foster Bros (Central Services) Ltd, part of Sears Group Plc, and finished his 'policing' career as an Insurance Investigator with Colin Farley and Associates Ltd, a firm of Chartered Loss Adjusters.

However, Jim still continued his association with matters police for several years after, by teaching GSCE Law at South Sefton Adult Education Centre.

This is the second book Jim has written, the first being "Memories of Mr Moonlight – A Tribute to Frankie Vaughan CBE."

ACKNOWLEDGEMENTS

My thanks and best wishes are due to the following for their help and assistance in the preparation of this book:-

    Marjorie Brunskill
    Bill Roberts
    Charlie Southern
    Eileen Brewer